ALMONDS

Contain healthy fats, fiber, protein, magnesium and vitamin E. Lowering blood sugar levels, reduce blood pressure and lower cholesterol levels.

TOMATOES

The Great source of the antioxidant lycopene, which has been linked to many health benefits, including reduced risk of heart disease and cancer.

KIWI

High in Vitamin C and dietary fiber. Can support heart health, digestive health, and immunity.

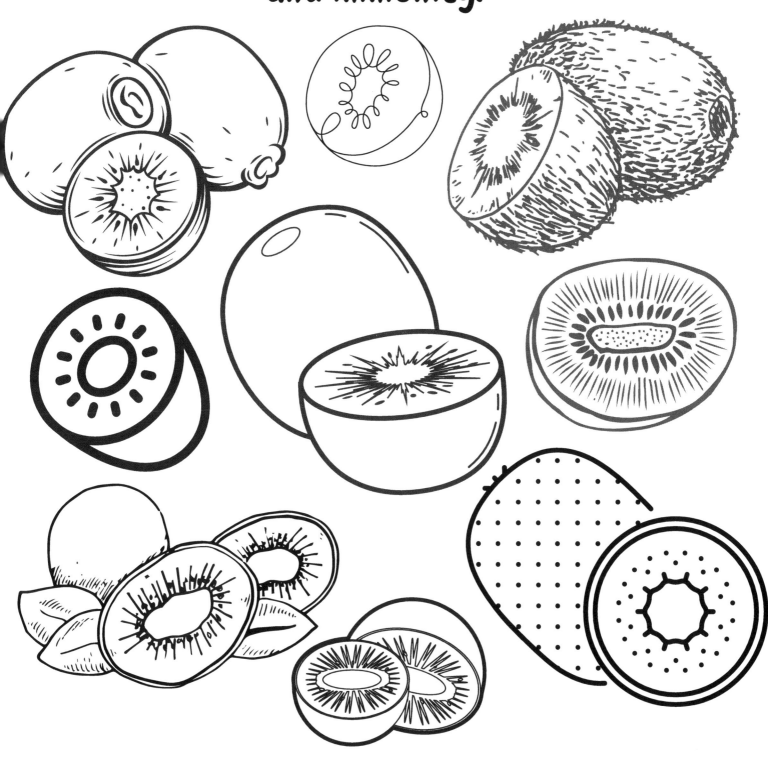

ONIONS

High in Quercetin it's a potent anti-inflammatory, it may help decrease heart disease risk factors.

QUINOA

Gluten-free, high in protein that contains sufficient amounts of all 9 essential amino acids Quercetin and Kaempferol.

MUSHROOM

Has Ergothioneine for boost immunity.

BROCCOLI

Has Sulforaphane for anti-cancer.

POTATO

Has Potassium for reduce blood pressure and water retention.

CABBAGE

Has Glucoraphanin that can reduce inflammation.

GARLIC

Has Inulin and Saponins for cancer prevention.

CARROT

Has Beta carotene
for good eyes and skin.

STRAWBERRY

Has Pelargonidin
for cardiovascular disease prevention.

BLUEBERRY

Has Anthocyanin can help heart health, bone strength, and mental health.

ORANGE

Has Vitamin C is necessary for the growth, and repair of all body tissues.

APPLE

Has Quercetin helped control blood sugar, and help prevent heart disease.

PASSION FRUIT

It contains high levels of vitamin A, which is important for skin, vision, and the immune system.

AVOCADO

Avocados are a source of vitamins C, E, K, and B6, niacin, folate, beneficial fats, which can help a person feel fuller between meals.

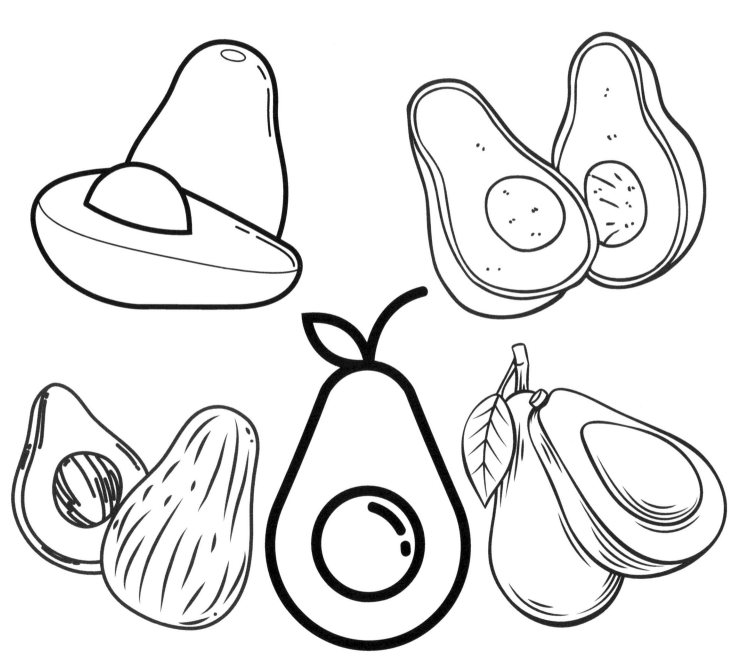

GINGER

Contains gingerol, aid digestion, reduce nausea, and help fight the flu and common cold.

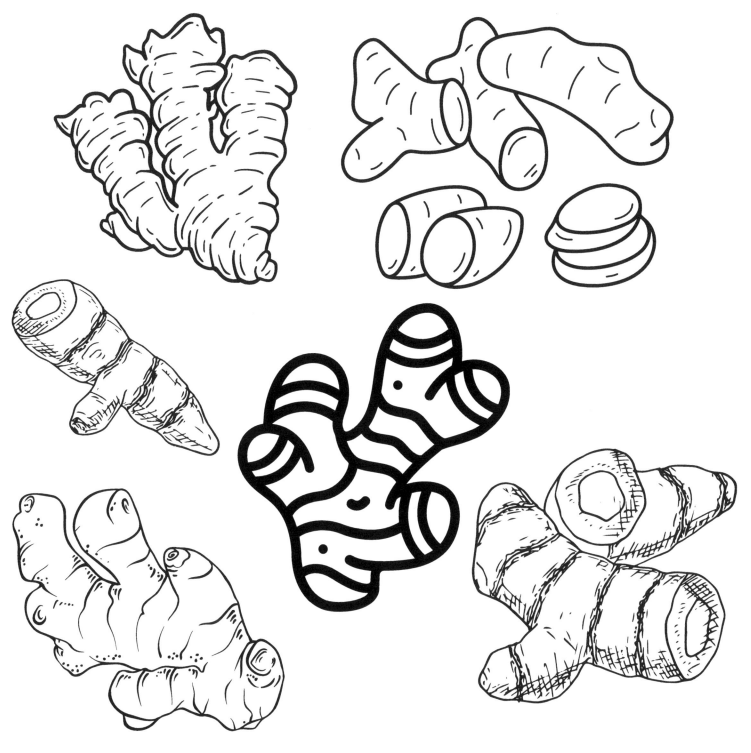

NATTO

Has Vitamin K2 prevention of osteoporosis as well as cardiovascular & coronary disease, kidney disorders, diabetes and cancer.

SOY

Soy is a high-quality protein and soy foods may reduce the risk of cardiovascular disease, stroke, coronary heart disease , some cancers as well as improving bone health.

KALE

Very high in Vitamin K, A, and C Kale is very high in nutrients and very low in calories, making it one of the most nutrient-dense foods on the planet.

COLLARD

Has Vitamins A, K, B-6, and C, calcium, iron, and magnesium that lowered cancer risk and improved heart health.

LETTUCE

High in a variety of essential vitamins and minerals, very low in calories.

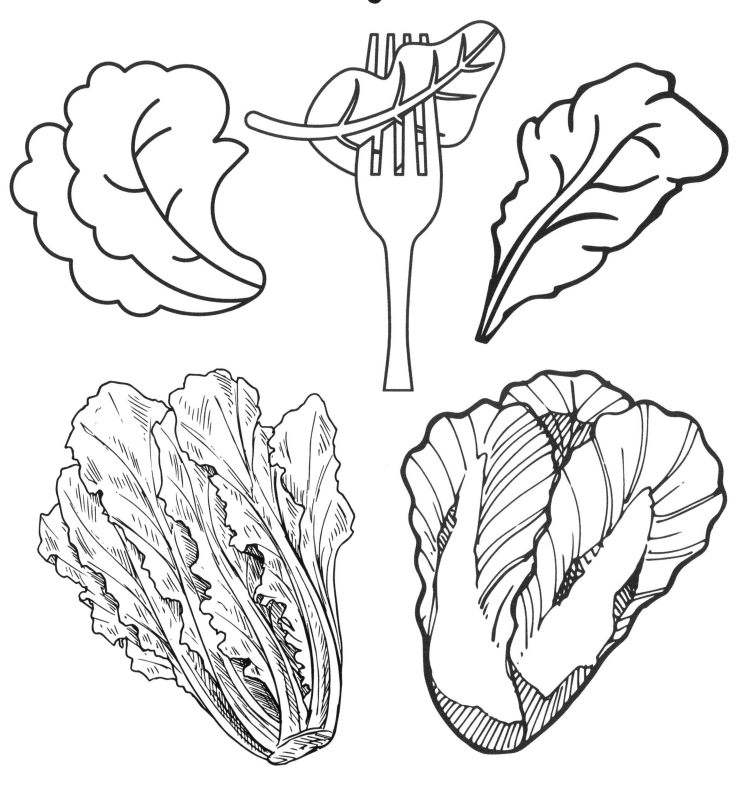

GRASS-FED BEEF

Has been found to be higher in vitamins A, E, and other antioxidants compared to grain fed beef

TURKEY

very rich source of protein, niacin, vitamin B6, and the amino acid tryptophan, it also contains zinc and vitamin B12.

OATS

Promotes healthy bacteria in your gut.
Lowers your chance of colon cancer.
Eases constipation.

PUMPKIN

Rich in Vitamin A. High Antioxidant Content May Reduce Your Risk of Chronic Diseases. Packs Vitamins That May Boost Immunity.

LEMON

Lemons are a good source of vitamin C.
Improve Digestive Health.
Support Heart Health.

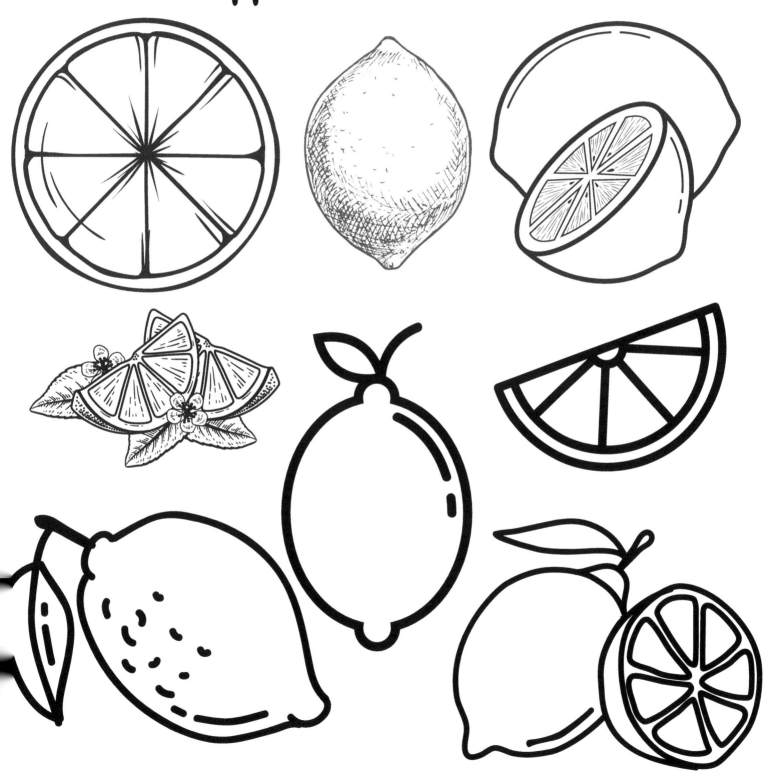

BANANAS

Contain potassium, folate, and antioxidants. All of these support heart health.

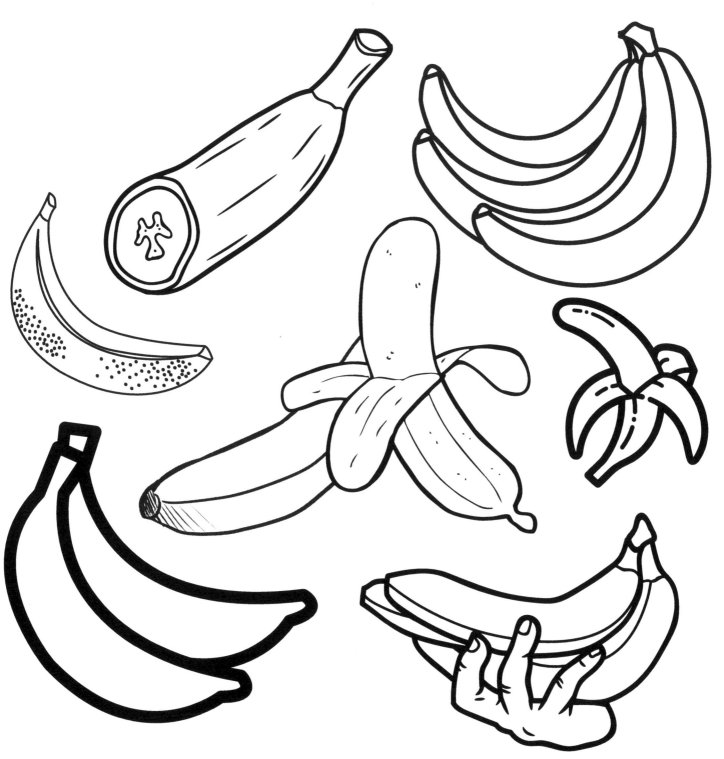

EGGS

High Protein. Whole eggs supply almost every nutrient you need.

WALNUTS

Decrease Inflammation. Promotes a Healthy Gut. Supports Healthy Aging.

ASPARAGUS

Great source of nutrients, including fiber, folate, and vitamins A, C, and K. Help weight loss, improved digestion,

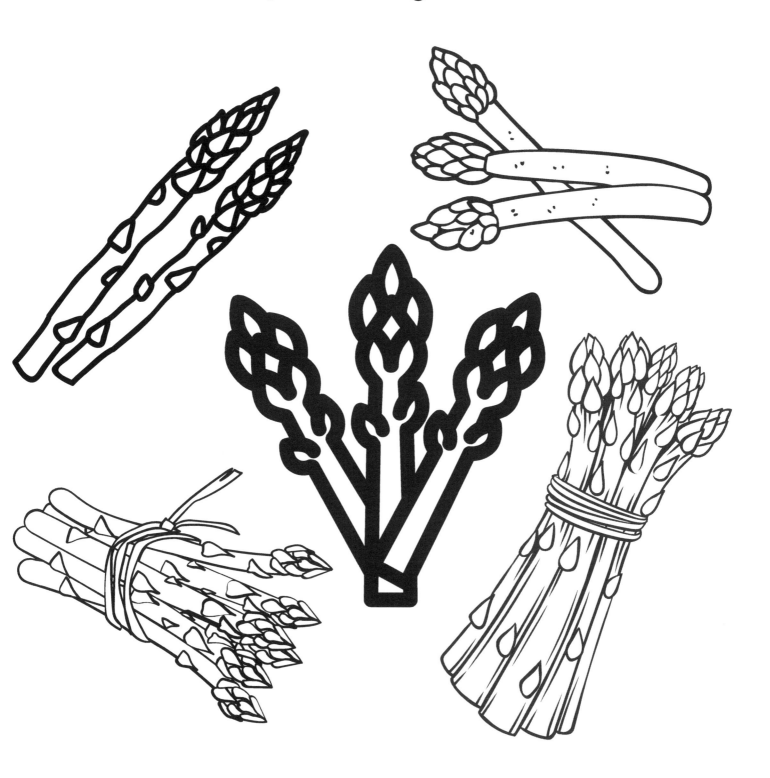

BELL PEPPERS

High in vitamin C and various carotenoids. Improved eye health and reduced the risk of several chronic diseases.

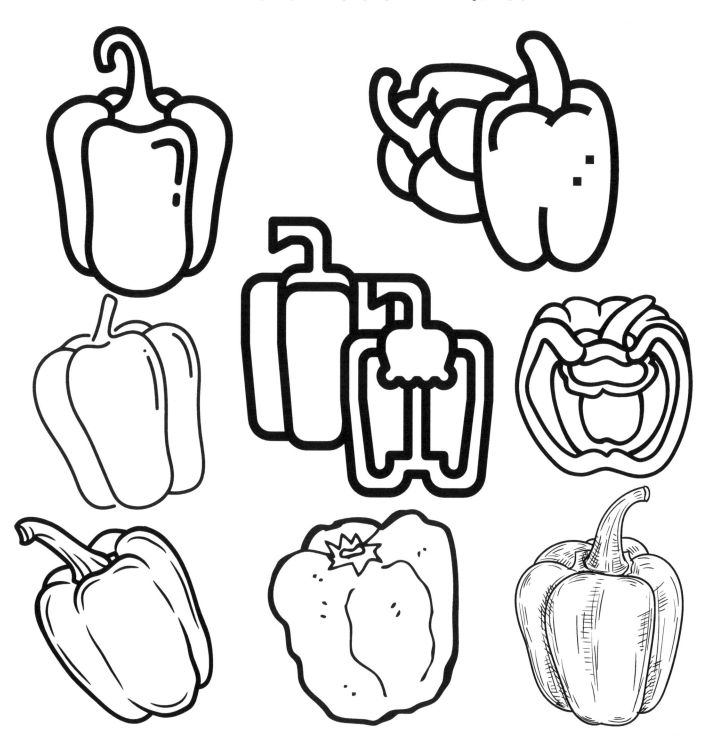

CAULIFLOWER

High in fiber and B-vitamins. It provides antioxidants and phytonutrients that can protect against cancer.

SALMON

Rich in Omega-3 fatty acids. These fatty acids are thought to contribute to a healthy heart and help maintain skin, joints and hormonal balance.

OATS

Lowers blood sugar levels.
Provides antioxidants.
Promotes healthy bacteria in your gut.

KIDNEY BEANS

High protein, fiber, and antioxidants.
Aiding weight management,

PINTO BEAN

CHICKPEAS

High protein and fiber. Aiding weight management,

LENTILS

TROPICAL FRUITS

High in Vitamin C and A Packed with Disease-Fighting Antioxidants.

PAPAYA

PINEAPPLE

PITAYA

RAMBUTAN

WATERMELON

Made in the USA
Coppell, TX
17 March 2022

75078625R00042